D0688597

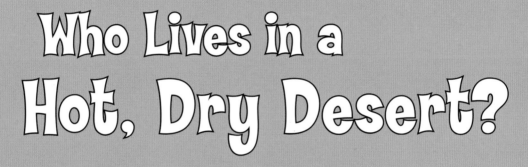

Who Lives in a Hot, Dry Desert?

Rachel Lynette

PowerKiDS press

New York

For Donny, who touched a cactus when we were young

Published in 2011 by The Rosen Publishing Group, Inc.
29 East 21st Street, New York, NY 10010

Copyright © 2011 by The Rosen Publishing Group, Inc.

All rights reserved. No part of this book may be reproduced in any form without permission in writing from the publisher, except by a reviewer.

First Edition

Editor: Joanne Randolph
Book Design: Greg Tucker
Photo Researcher: Jessica Gerweck

Photo Credits: Cover, pp. 4, 5, 6, 7, 8, 9, 10, 11, 14–15, 16–17, 19, 22 Shutterstock.com; p. 12 © FLPA/Chris Mattison/age fotostock; p. 13 © www.iStockphoto.com/Deanna Quinton Larson; p. 18 Owen Newman/Getty Images; p. 20 © John Cancalosi/age fotostock; p. 21 Purestock/Getty Images.

Library of Congress Cataloging-in-Publication Data

Lynette, Rachel.
  Who lives in a hot, dry desert? / Rachel Lynette. — 1st ed.
      p. cm. — (Exploring habitats)
  Includes index.
  ISBN 978-1-4488-0679-9 (library binding) — ISBN 978-1-4488-1285-1 (pbk.) — ISBN 978-1-4488-1286-8 (6-pack)
  1. Desert animals—Juvenile literature. I. Title.
  QL116.L96 2011
  591.754—dc22

                            2010000241

Manufactured in the United States of America

CPSIA Compliance Information: Batch #WS10PK: For Further Information contact Rosen Publishing, New York, New York at 1-800-237-9932

Contents

Deserts are the driest places on Earth. That is because very little rain falls in a desert. In some deserts it does not rain at all for years at a time. Most deserts are very hot during the day, but at night they can get very cold.

In the Mojave Desert in the United States, grass, small trees, and bushes grow. All these plants need little water.

The United States has four large deserts. These are the Mojave, Sonoran, Great Basin, and Chihuahuan deserts. The largest desert completely inside the United States is the Great Basin.

4

The largest desert on Earth is the Sahara, in Africa. It is almost as big as the United States. In parts of the Sahara, you can walk hundreds of miles (km) and see nothing but sand. Some deserts are sandy, like parts of the Sahara, while others are rocky.

Large dunes, or hills of sand, are made by the wind on the Sahara. The shape of this sandy land is always changing!

5

Beating the Heat

The hot, dry desert is a hard place to live. Many plants and animals do well in the desert **environment**, though. They have **adaptations** that help them live there.

Desert plants do not need much water. A cactus

Many desert plants are prickly so that they do not get too much sun on their leaves. This also helps keep animals from eating them.

can store a lot of water. It has no leaves and small roots. There are also grasses, bushes, and small trees in the desert. Some desert plants may have one root that is really long. This root goes deep into the soil to find water.

The needles and deep valleys on this cactus help give it some shade from the hot sun.

Desert animals have adapted to hot weather, too. Some stay underground during the day. They come out only at night. Many desert animals are also light in color. This helps them take in less heat and hide from **predators**.

This lizard is light in color. This helps it hide in the dull colors of the desert. It also helps keep the sun from overheating its body.

7

Desert Mammals

There are lots of **mammals** in the desert. Small mammals, such as jackrabbits and ground squirrels, search for grasses, seeds, and other plants. They get all the water they need from the plants they eat. Larger mammals, such

Jackrabbits have great hearing, but their ears have another job, too. They help cool the rabbit's blood on hot days.

as coyotes and desert jackals, eat these smaller animals.

Peccaries live in deserts in the southern parts of North America and in Central America. One of the foods they like best is the prickly pear. This is a good food for them, since it has a lot of water inside it!

8

Coyotes live in deserts and many other places in North America. They do well in many places because they eat almost anything and can change quickly to fit new living conditions.

Camels live in the deserts of Africa and Asia. These animals can drink huge amounts of water and save it in their stomachs. A camel can store a quarter of its body weight in water!

Fennecs' ears work the same way jackrabbits' do. They hear very well and help keep the animal cool. Fennecs live in the Sahara.

Meerkats are a kind of mongoose. They live together in large groups of up to 40 animals. They live in the Kalahari Desert, in Africa, where they dig large burrows with many tunnels and rooms.

Here some meerkats stand on their back legs to take a look around. The dark rings around their eyes help keep their eyes safe from the bright desert sun.

Meerkats eat insects, spiders, small **rodents**, lizards, eggs, and even scorpions that they find in the sand. Meerkats look for food during the day. While the meerkats eat, one of them acts as a guard. The guard stands up on its back legs and looks for predators, such as eagles or jackals. If the guard sees a predator, it whistles loudly. When the other meerkats hear the whistle, they all jump into nearby burrows.

The Kalahari Desert is in southern Africa. Some grasses, bushes, and small trees grow there.

Reptiles in the Sand

The desert is home to many different **cold-blooded reptiles**. Reptiles count on sunlight and the warm ground to heat up their bodies. Snakes and lizards spend the morning hours basking in the sun to warm up after a cool night.

The sandfish lives in the sands of the Sahara and in deserts as far east as Iran. It does not use its legs while under the sand. Instead, it moves its body like a snake.

Even reptiles must find shelter during the hottest part of the day. Desert turtles and tortoises dig burrows. Snakes and lizards bury themselves in the sand or find shade under rocks.

Most lizards eat insects and other small animals. The sandfish, or desert skink, of Africa moves like a fish beneath the sand and hunts for insects. The sand viper, a kind of snake, hides under the sand, too. When an animal comes close, it jumps out and has some lunch!

The desert tortoise lives in the Sonoran and Mojave deserts. This kind of tortoise eats mostly plants.

13

Noisy Rattlers

What makes a rattlesnake **rattle**? A rattlesnake has rings of **keratin** at the end of its tail. Your fingernails are also made from keratin. When a rattlesnake moves its tail very quickly, the **vibrations** cause the rings to hit

Rattlesnakes do not lay eggs, as most other snakes do. Instead they give birth to live babies.

each other. This makes a rattling sound. Rattlesnakes hunt rodents, ground squirrels, rabbits, and other animals. A rattlesnake can hunt in the dark because it can sense the heat coming from its prey's body. It kills its prey with **venom** from its sharp fangs. Rattlesnakes hunt only when they are hungry. An adult rattlesnake needs to eat only about once every two weeks!

Monsters in the Desert

A Gila monster is not really a monster. It is a kind of lizard. Many kinds of lizards, such as horned lizards and desert iguanas, call deserts home. Gila monsters live in the deserts of the southwestern United States.

Gila monsters have black bodies with orange, pink, or yellow markings. They can spend up to 95 percent of their lives in their burrows!

A Gila monster is about as long as your arm.

Gila monsters move slowly, so they must sneak up on their prey. They eat baby rodents, rabbits, and smaller lizards. A Gila monster kills its prey with venom. A Gila monster may chew on its prey to put more venom into the **wound**. Once the animal is dead, though, the Gila monster swallows the prey whole!

So Many Birds

Many different species, or kinds, of birds live in the desert. Some birds live in the desert all year long. Others **migrate** to the desert for only part of the year.

This elf owl peeks out from a hole in a saguaro cactus. Elf owls are about the size of a sparrow and eat bugs, such as moths, crickets, scorpions, and beetles.

The Gila woodpecker spends its whole life in the desert. Rather than pecking a hole in a tree, the Gila woodpecker makes its nest in a large cactus! Later, other birds, such as the tiny elf owl, live in holes the woodpeckers have left behind.

Eagles, hawks, and other large birds fly high above looking for prey. Turkey vultures look for dead animals to eat. They use their strong sense of smell to find rotting meat.

The wings of a turkey vulture are nearly 6 feet (2 m) from tip to tip. The part of its brain that makes sense of smells is much larger than that of other birds.

Roadrunners can fly, but they almost never do. Instead they run. A roadrunner can run up to 17 miles per hour (27 km/h). That is one fast bird!

Roadrunners hunt for many small animals in the desert.

This greater roadrunner has caught a rattlesnake. Roadrunners do not chew their food. Instead they swallow it whole.

They like rattlesnakes best, though. A roadrunner kills a rattlesnake by grabbing it by the tail with its beak and hitting the snake's head against the ground. Roadrunners also eat insects, lizards, rodents, and smaller birds.

Pairs of roadrunners build their nests in bushes, low trees, or cacti. Both the male and the female gather sticks for the nest, but only the female builds it. Both parents care for the eggs and the baby birds.

Roadrunners lay between three and six eggs. Babies hatch, or break free from the egg, after about 20 days.

Full of Life

It might look like nothing lives in the desert, but now you know that is not true. Insects, scorpions, and countless animals, such as desert tortoises, packrats, and jerboas, hide under the sand and rocks and in burrows.

Bearded dragons live in deserts in central Australia. They can change their skin color from light to dark to help them stay cool and to hide from enemies.

As the Sun sets, the desert comes alive. Animals come out to look for food and find **mates**. The desert is full of life, you just need to know when and where to look!

Glossary

adaptations (a-dap-TAY-shunz) Changes in animals that help them stay alive.

cold-blooded (KOHLD-bluh-did) Having body heat that changes with the heat around the body.

environment (en-VY-ern-ment) All the living things and conditions of a place.

keratin (KEHR-uh-tun) Matter that is found in people's hair and nails and in animal fur, scales, and horns.

mammals (MA-mulz) Warm-blooded animals that have backbones and hair, breathe air, and feed milk to their young.

mates (MAYTS) Male and female animals that come together to make babies.

migrate (MY-grayt) To move from one place to another.

predators (PREH-duh-terz) Animals that kill other animals for food.

rattle (RA-tul) To make repeated short, sharp noises.

reptiles (REP-tylz) Cold-blooded animals with thin, dry pieces of skin called scales.

rodents (ROH-dents) Animals with gnawing teeth, such as mice.

venom (VEH-num) A poison passed by one animal into another through a bite or a sting.

vibrations (vy-BRAY-shunz) Fast movements up and down or back and forth.

wound (WOOND) A place where the body is hurt and bleeding.

Index

A
Africa, 5, 9–10, 13
animal(s), 6–10, 13–14,
     17, 19–20, 22

C
cactus, 6, 18, 21
Chihuahuan Desert, 4

D
day, 4, 7, 10, 12

E
Earth, 4–5

G
Great Basin Desert, 4

K
keratin, 14

M
mates, 22
Mojave Desert, 4

N
night, 4, 7, 12

P
plants, 6, 8
predators, 7, 11

R
rattle, 14
roadrunner(s), 20–21

rodents, 10, 14, 16, 20

S
Sahara, 5
sand, 5, 10, 12–13, 22
soil, 6
Sonoran Desert, 4

U
United States, 4–5, 16

V
venom, 15, 17
vibrations, 14

W
water, 6, 8–9

Web Sites

Due to the changing nature of Internet links, PowerKids Press has developed an online list of Web sites related to the subject of this book. This site is updated regularly. Please use this link to access the list:
www.powerkidslinks.com/explore/hdd/